THE SEVERE STYLE OF ANCIENT GREEK ART

ART HISTORY FOR KIDS
Children's Art Books

BABY PROFESSOR

EDUCATION KIDS

Speedy Publishing LLC
40 E. Main St. #1156
Newark, DE 19711
www.speedypublishing.com

In this book, we're going to talk about the Severe Style of Ancient Greek art. So, let's get right to it!

The Ancient Greeks became well known for the perfect details they highlighted in their art forms. During the Classical Era from 490 to 450 BC, they developed a unique style, which modern art historians would call the *"Severe Style."*

In order to understand this shift in their design style, it should be compared to the design style that they displayed in the previous period of history called the Archaic Period.

Kritios Boy - Statue of an ephebe, perhaps an athlete, 480 BC.

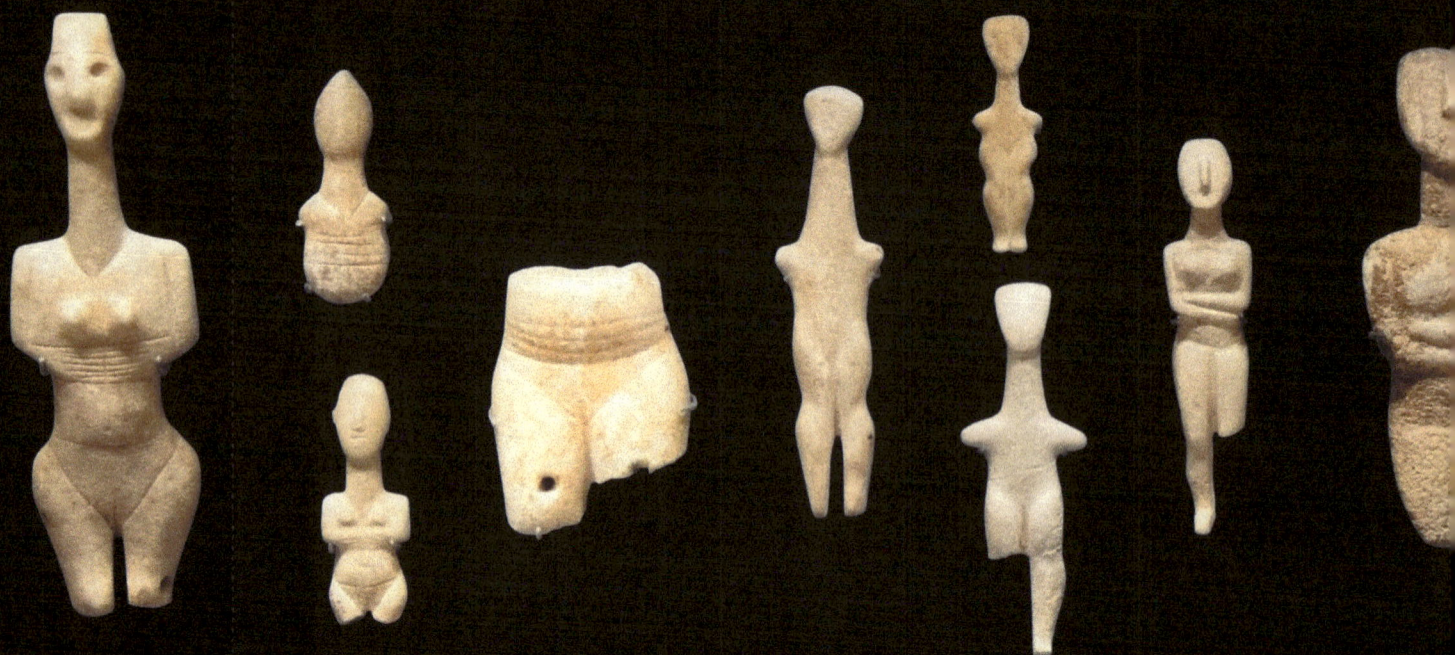

Marble figurines from Cyclades. Early Bronze Age, 3200 – 2300 BC.

GREEK ART IN THE ARCHAIC PERIOD

Around 1000 BC, the Greeks began to produce life-size and larger-than-life-size sculptures made of stone. It was the first time they had done this since they produced the Stone-Age statues called the Cycladic sculptures around 2500 BC. The Cycladic sculptures were made of marble and were generally used in tombs. The only facial features sculpted on Cycladic sculptures were the noses. They look like modern abstract art today.

During the Archaic Period, between 800 BC to 479 BC, Greek sculptors wanted their statues to stand upright and not have to lean against another structure or wall. During this time period, many Greek men were in Egypt working as paid soldiers. They were able to observe how the Egyptians created their statues.

Kouros (archaic greek period).

One technique that they learned from the Egyptians was to use a triangularly shaped face with two triangles positioned upside down on either side of the face to create the hair. The limestone used wasn't as strong as marble or granite so it was important to not have the face supported only by the neck.

Relief with Heroes and Worshipers, archaic period.

Another idea that they took from the Egyptians was to have one leg positioned a little in front of the other. This also helped to make the statue more balanced and less prone to falling over. One major difference was that the Egyptians always showed clothes on the bodies of their sculptures. The Greeks thought that the male form was sacred and that the gods and goddesses admired it, so they created their male sculptures without any clothes on.

The Kore of Euthydikos, 490 BC.

The women's sculptures were dressed and their skirts were created to hit the ground so it helped the statue to be stable. In the city-state of Athens, girl statues were made so that they were quietly standing still, but in the city-state of Sparta where they encouraged women athletes, their sculptures sometimes showed women in athletic poses. Most of the statues looked alike and had similar features. They had stiff, formal poses and most of them had their arms held at their sides.

The peplos kore, circa 530 BC.

These statues of the Archaic period were called *"Kouros"* meaning *"Boy"* for the boy statues and *"Kore"* meaning *"Girl"* for the girl statues.

Although the paint did not survive over the many centuries, most Greek statues, like the ones in Egypt, were painted like mannequins so they would look more like real people.

Kouros from thebes.

The Archaic Period was a very uncertain time in Greek culture, so their statues played against this uncertainty by being very consistent and similar time after time. The Persians were finally defeated at the battle of Plataea and the battle of Mykale in 479 BC and this was the dawn of a new era for the Greek culture.

Kore no. 675

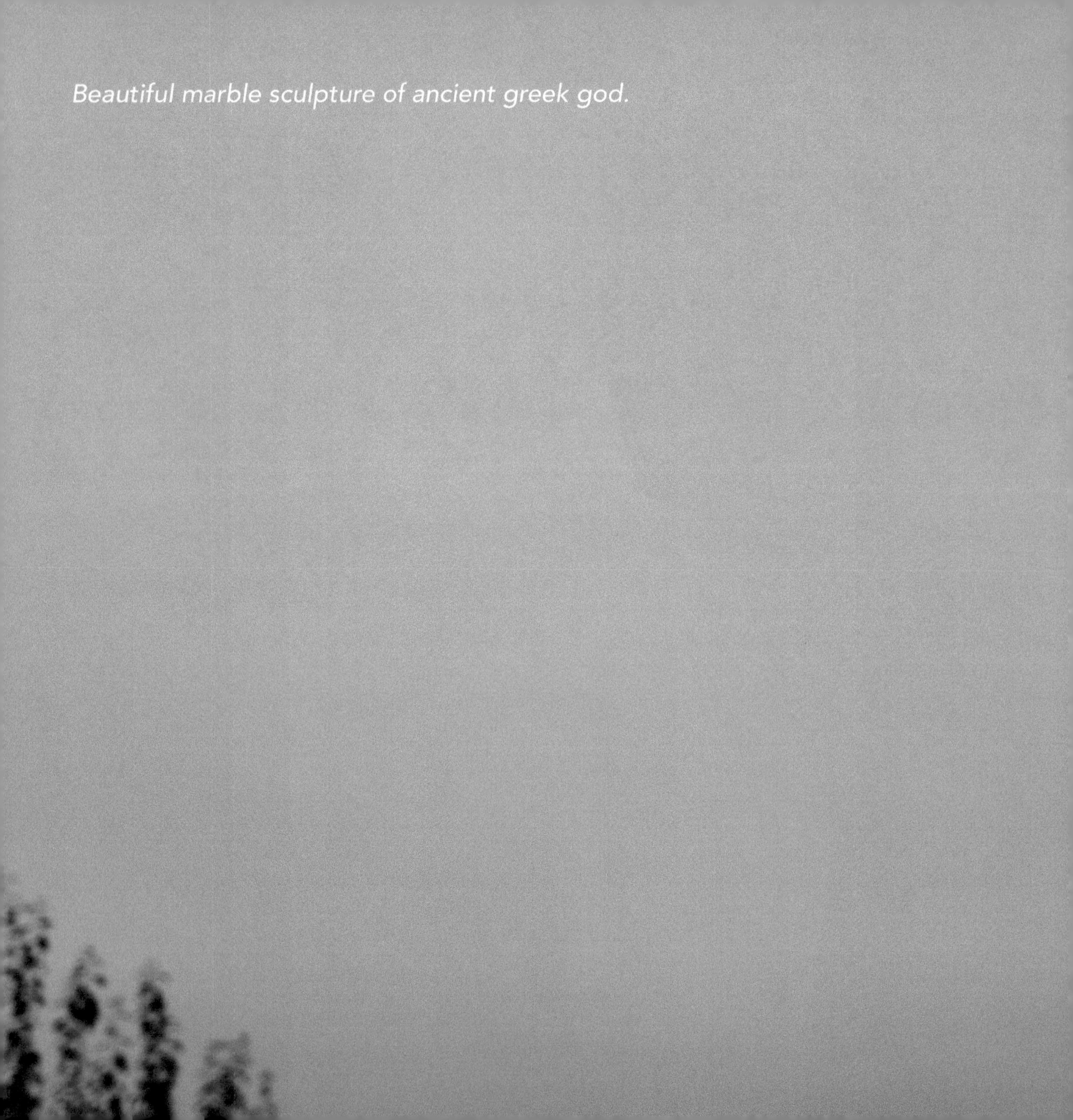

Beautiful marble sculpture of ancient greek god.

GREEK ART IN THE EARLY CLASSICAL PERIOD

The stiff, consistent style of the Archaic Period began to change and a new style emerged during the Early Classical Period from 490 to 450 BC. The new style quickly replaced the style that had been used before. Art historians later called it the *"Severe Style."*

During this time period, sculptors worked to make their statues more realistic. The bones and muscles of the body were closer to the way the anatomy of a person really looks. There was more emotion in their faces although the Greek straight-line profile was idealized and hair was sometimes represented with just a few strands of curls.

"Blond Kouros" head, fragment from the statue of a youth. Marble with traces of brown-blond painting on the hair, ca. 490–480 BC.

One of the biggest shifts was the representation of movement. These statues didn't just stand or sit still. They threw spears, rode horses, or drove chariots. Their arms and legs were in full movement. The Greeks had started this trend earlier on the vases they painted and now the sculptors were imitating this look as well.

Goddess seated on a throne (Persephone)

Another big shift was that, unlike the Archaic Period where most of the statues were similar-looking youths, the Early Classical Period saw sculptors creating sculptures of men, women, and children in all age ranges. The sculptors had made many improvements on how to make statues that would balance. During this time, they also began working in bronze, which was much lighter and more flexible than stone.

Valley of the temples.

Erechtheion with Porch of the Caryatids, Greece.

PERFECTION AND FREEDOM OF EXPRESSION

During the *"Severe Style"* time period, the Greek sculptors wanted to show the idealized, perfect human form. Unlike Roman sculptors, they didn't want to represent human beings in any way that would make them seem imperfect. Their facial features were perfect and so were their bodies. The Greeks reached a peak of excellence in art that captured the beauty of the human form in a way that had not been seen before.

This emphasis on the proportions of the figure, the graceful movements and poise of the figure, and the depiction of the perfect human bodies has made their art easy to recognize. They sculpted these monuments to perfection in both stone and bronze. They used a lost-wax process to create multiple copies of bronze statues. This is not a simple process. It requires a lot of artistic skill to achieve the perfection that the Greeks wanted to display.

Apollo statue.

This desire for perfection was expressed with total joy and freedom of movement. Imagine a little child posing for a photo portrait. She is standing straight and rigid and the photo is taken. She looks really uncomfortable and her energy is bound up. But then, the photographer gets the same child to go outdoors and she starts chasing a butterfly.

Discobolous 7

Now the photographer takes these shots of the child running and playing. These photographs are filled with joy and zest for life. This is a good way to think of the difference in the way the human form was presented in the Archaic Period compared to the Early Classical Period.

Vase with a greek historic scene.

The Greeks had mastered the way the muscles in the body play against each other with tension and relaxation and this is what gave their statues the natural balance that is present in the human body. The human body was a subject of admiration and worthy of being put up on a pedestal. The statues took command of the space around them like never before.

Perseus with the Head of Medusa.

Parthenon Frieze.

FAMOUS SCULPTORS OF THE EARLY CLASSICAL PERIOD

Greek artists were very proud of their work and frequently signed their finished art. Some of these original pieces of art have survived. Other pieces we know about through historical works and reproductions.

PHIDIAS

Perhaps the most famous sculptor of this era was Phidias. He created the huge statue of the goddess Athena in 438 BC. It was a chryselephantine statue, which simply means it was a statue covered in real gold and ivory. His goddess stood in the famous Parthenon in Athens. He also created the chryselephantine statue of the god Zeus in 456 BC. It was a gigantic statue that was housed at the Temple of Zeus located at Olympia. This statue was one of the ancient world's seven wonders.

Athena Varvakeion, small Roman replica of the Athena Parthenos by Phidias.

POLYKLEITOS

Polykleitos created a great sculpture called Doryphoros, which was a man carrying a spear on his left shoulder. He meant for this sculpture to embody the principles he wrote about in a manuscript called the Kanon, which outlined how to sculpt with perfect proportions.

The Doryphoros by Polykleitos.

KRESILAS

Another important sculptor was Kresilas. He created a statue of Pericles, the famous Greek statesman, in 425 BC. This statue made an already famous man even more famous and was copied for decades by other sculptors.

Ancient marble portrait bust of Pericles

PRAXITELES

The sculptor Praxiteles was known for creating the first female sculpture that had no clothes. This was the sculpture of the goddess of love, Aphrodite.

Cnidus Aphrodite. Marble, by Praxiteles

KALLIMACHOS

The sculptor Kallimachos is thought to have created the dancing figures of the Corinthian capital, which were later copied by the Romans.

Dancing maenad.

Sculptors were often permanently employed at the sites of the Greek sanctuaries. Phidias is known to have had a workshop at Olympia. Archaeologists have found clay molds in these locations. It's also known that the sculptors were helped by cleaners and bronze polishers. The Greeks wanted their bronze to have its shiny brass, reddish color and not get the patina of dark green from weathering.

"Exaltation de la Fleur" (exaltation of the flower),
fragment from a grave stele, ca. 470–460 BC.

The Greeks strove for artistic perfection during the Early Classical period. When they were conquered by the Romans in 146 BC, the Roman conquerers absorbed much of the Grecian artistic style into their own culture.

Awesome! Now you know more about the Severe Style of art in Ancient Greece. You can find more Art History books from Baby Professor by searching the website of your favorite book retailer.

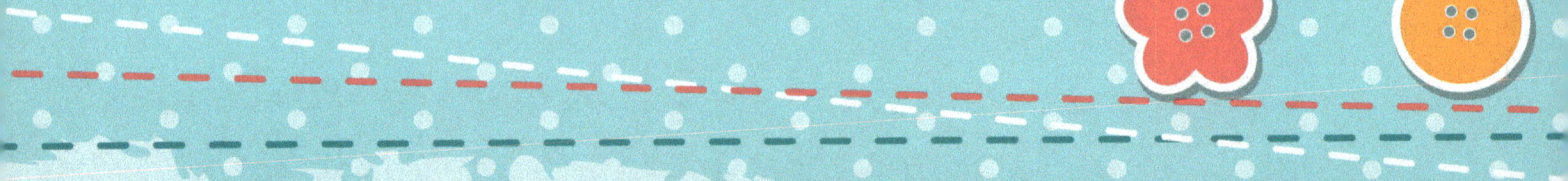

Visit

BABY PROFESSOR
EDUCATION KIDS

www.BabyProfessorBooks.com

to download Free Baby Professor eBooks
and view our catalog of new and exciting
Children's Books

9 798869 402974